THE TOMB IS EMPTY

Chloe E. Gore

My name is Mary Magdalene, and I want to tell you the story of Easter.

It happened long ago—before phones, cars, or even shoes! Back then, Jesus lived among us, and this is his story.

I lived in the small town of Bethany with my sister Martha and my brother Lazarus. We had many friends, and one of them was Jesus.

One day, Lazarus fell ill. Everyone was sad because he was kind and full of joy.

Martha cried, and I tried to comfort her.

We believed only Jesus could help, so we quickly sent him a letter, asking him to heal our brother. Then, we waited anxiously for two days.

And guess what? Jesus came!

Not on a horse or in a carriage, but on a donkey.

But since he didn't have a watch or a phone, he arrived too late—Lazarus had already died.

But imagine our surprise when Jesus rolled away the big stone and called, 'Lazarus, come out!'

And just like that, he got up—like waking from a nap! That's when we truly understood the power of love and faith. Jesus smiled, and we jumped for joy!

A few days later, we traveled with Jesus to Jerusalem! The city was filled with excitement—people sang joyful songs as Jesus rode his donkey.

We walked beside him, carrying not just the joy of Lazarus' healing but also the light of faith and hope in our hearts.

As we entered Jerusalem, the people rushed out, welcoming him like a king. But Jesus, always humble, reminded them he was not a king. They laid down their cloaks and waved palm branches, celebrating his arrival.

His smile warmed their hearts, and everyone felt joy, knowing he had come to help and share his love.

As evening came, Jesus and his twelve apostles gathered for a special supper to celebrate Passover. They met in a house in Jerusalem.

Before they ate, he took off his coat, filled a bowl with water, and gently washed his friends' feet, showing how important it is to be kind and help each other.

Then Jesus turned to his disciples and said,
'See this bread and wine?'
'Eat this bread and remember me.'
He shared the bread with his friends.
'Now drink this,' he said.
'Drink this wine and remember me.'
And his friends drank from the cup he gave them.

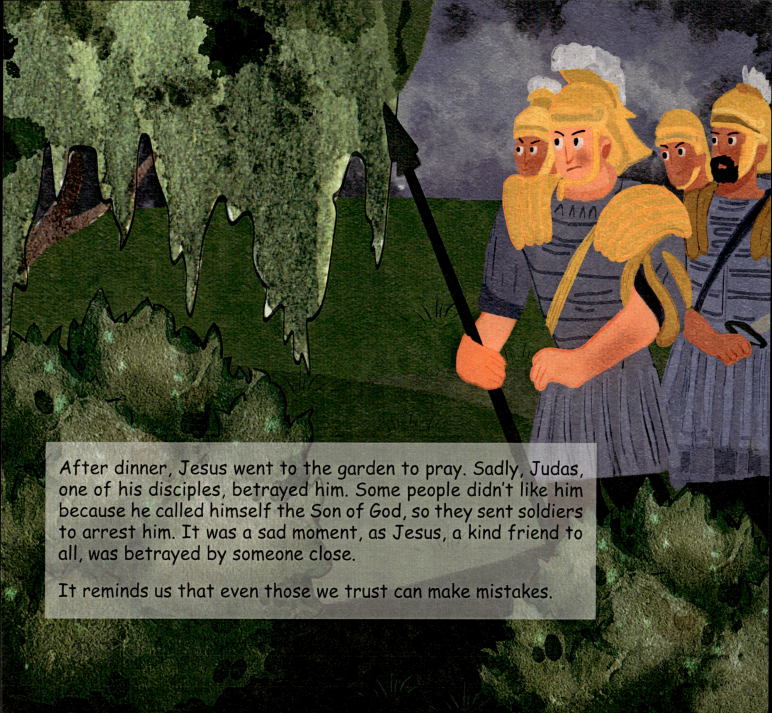

After dinner, Jesus went to the garden to pray. Sadly, Judas, one of his disciples, betrayed him. Some people didn't like him because he called himself the Son of God, so they sent soldiers to arrest him. It was a sad moment, as Jesus, a kind friend to all, was betrayed by someone close.

It reminds us that even those we trust can make mistakes.

After they captured him, they took him to a court. They accused him of many things, but all of it was lies.

Some people who didn't like Jesus made up stories, hoping to have him declared guilty.

Later, they placed him on a big wooden cross to die.
It was very hard for all of us, especially for me.

But Jesus said this was his plan to help everyone.
We were sad, but we also had hope, believing that
something important would happen.

I thought I had lost a friend, but on the third day, when I went with my friends to his tomb, **it was empty!**

An angel, glowing and beautiful, told us Jesus had risen from the dead, just like he said he would!

It was amazing, and we could hardly believe it was real.

But that's not all! Suddenly, I heard a voice I knew so well—it was Jesus! He appeared, alive and shining with light and joy.

All our sadness turned into joy. Jesus promised to always be with us, and our hearts were filled with happiness!

Jesus asked us to share the good news, so we went from house to house, telling everyone.